Manatees/Manatíes

By Valerie J. Weber

Reading Consultant: Susan Nations, M.Ed.,
author/literacy coach/consultant in literacy development/

Consultora de lectura: Susan Nations, M.Ed.,
autora/tutora de alfabetización/consultora de desarrollo de lectoescritura

WEEKLY READER®
PUBLISHING

Please visit our web site at www.garethstevens.com.
For a free catalog describing our list of high-quality books,
call 1-800-542-2595 (USA) or 1-800-387-3178 (Canada).
Our fax: 1-877-542-2596

Library of Congress Cataloging-in-Publication Data

Weber, Valerie.
      (Manatees. Spanish & English)
      Manatees = Manatíes / by/por Valerie J. Weber.
          p. cm. — (Animals that live in the ocean = Animales que viven en el océano)
      Includes bibliographical references and index.
      ISBN-10: 0-8368-9247-X   ISBN-13: 978-0-8368-9247-5 (lib. bdg.)
      ISBN-10: 0-8368-9346-8   ISBN-13: 978-0-8368-9346-5 (softcover)
      1. Manatees—Juvenile literature. I. Title. II. Title: Manatíes.
  QL737.S63W4318   2009
  599.55—dc22   2008016889

This edition first published in 2009 by
Weekly Reader® Books
An Imprint of Gareth Stevens Publishing
1 Reader's Digest Road
Pleasantville, NY 10570-7000 USA

Senior Managing Editor: Lisa M. Herrington
Senior Editor: Barbara Bakowski
Creative Director: Lisa Donovan
Designer: Alexandria Davis
Cover Designer: Amelia Favazza, *Studio Montage*
Photo Researcher: Diane Laska-Swanke
Translation: Tatiana Acosta and Guillermo Gutiérrez

Photo Credits: Cover © Herb Segars/Animals Animals; pp. 1, 5, 9, 13, 15, 17, 19 © SeaPics.com; p. 7
© Steven David Miller/naturepl.com; p. 11 © Douglas Faulkner/Photo Researchers, Inc.;
p. 21 © Jeffrey Greenberg/Photo Researchers, Inc

Printed in the United States of America

1 2 3 4 5 6 7 8 9 10 09 08

Table of Contents

- - - - - - - - - - - - -

Contenido

Boldface words appear in the glossary./
Las palabras en **negrita** aparecen en el glosario.

Manatees on the Move

The manatee (MA-nuh-tee) swims slowly. It is looking for food to eat. It curls its upper lip around a plant. The manatee pulls the plant into its mouth.

Manatíes en movimiento

El manatí nada lentamente. Está buscando algo que comer. Agarra una planta con su labio superior y se la lleva a la boca.

A manatee looks a bit like a seal.
The manatee's long, plump body
ends in a rounded tail. Two
flippers at the front of the body
help the manatee steer.

- - - - - - - - - - - - - -

Un manatí se parece un poco
a un foca. Su cuerpo, largo y
rollizo, acaba en una cola
redondeada. Dos **aletas** en la
parte delantera le permiten
cambiar de dirección.

tail/
cola

flippers/
aletas

Manatees push through the water with their tails. They can roll over from head to tail. They can even swim upside down!

- - - - - - - - - - - - - - -

Los manatíes avanzan en el agua impulsándose con la cola. Pueden darse vuelta. ¡Pueden hasta nadar panza arriba!

Food and Flippers

A manatee eats only plants. The animal's flat teeth grind up the plants. As its teeth wear out, the manatee grows new teeth.

- - - - - - - - - - - - - -

Aletas y alimentos

Un manatí sólo come plantas. Los dientes planos del animal trituran las plantas. A medida que los dientes se le desgastan, le salen dientes nuevos.

A manatee's flippers are shaped like paddles. The animal uses its flippers to swim and get food. The manatee digs up plant roots with its flippers.

Las aletas de un manatí tienen forma de remos. El animal las usa para nadar y buscar comida. El manatí escarba con las aletas para desenterrar raíces.

Unlike a fish, a manatee breathes air. It sticks its short **snout** out of the water to breathe. Manatees often sleep near the surface of the water.

- - - - - - - - - - - - - - -

A diferencia de los peces, los manatíes respiran fuera del agua. Para respirar, sacan su corto **hocico**. Los manatíes suelen dormir cerca de la superficie del agua.

snout/
hocico

Baby Manatees

A baby manatee is called a **calf**. It drinks milk from its mother's body. The calf can also eat plants soon after birth.

- - - - - - - - - - - - - -

Pequeños manatíes

La **cría** de manatí bebe leche del cuerpo de la madre. También puede comer plantas poco después de nacer.

calf/
cría

Manatees and their babies make sounds to each other. They chirp, whistle, and squeal.

- - - - - - - - - - - - - -

Los manatíes y sus crías se comunican con sonidos como chirridos, silbidos y chillidos.

Manatees in Danger

Manatees are in danger from people. Boats sometimes hit manatees. Some people are trying to save manatees. They put up signs to warn boaters that manatees may be nearby.

- - - - - - - - - - - - - - -

Manatíes en peligro

Los seres humanos son un peligro para los manatíes. A veces, estos animales chocan con los botes. Para tratar de salvarlos, algunas personas ponen carteles para avisar a quienes van en bote de que hay manatíes cerca.

Glossary/Glosario

calf: a baby manatee or other animal

flippers: broad, flat body parts used
for swimming

snout: the front part of an animal's head, including
the nose

— – — – — – — – — – — – —

aletas: partes del cuerpo anchas y planas que sirven
para nadar

cría: manatí u otro animal cuando es joven

hocico: parte delantera de la cabeza de un
animal, incluyendo la nariz

For More Information/Más información

Books/Libros

Manatees. New Naturebooks (series). Mary Ann McDonald (The Child's World, 2007)

What Sea Animals Eat/¿Qué comen los animales del mar? Nature's Food Chains/Las cadenas alimentarias en la naturaleza (series). Joanne Mattern (Gareth Stevens, 2007)

Web Sites/Páginas web

Caribbean Environment Program: Manatees and Dugongs/ Programa Ambiental del Caribe: Manatíes y dugongos
www.cep.unep.org/kids/cb01.html
See a slide show on manatees and dugongs./Vean una serie de fotografías sobre los manatíes y los dugongos.

Jonathan Bird's Blue World: Swimming With Sea Cows/El mundo azul de Jonathan Bird: Nadando con las vacas marinas
www.blueworldtv.com/video_html/9_manatees.htm
Watch a video on manatees./Miren un video sobre los manatíes.

Index/Índice

About the Author

A writer and editor for 25 years, Valerie Weber especially loves working in children's publishing. The variety of topics is endless, from weird animals to making movies. It is her privilege to try to engage children in their world through books.

- - - - - - - - - - - - - - -

Información sobre la autora

A Valerie Weber, que ha sido escritora y editora durante 25 años, le gusta sobre todo trabajar en libros infantiles. La variedad de temas es inagotable: desde insólitos animales hasta cómo se hace una película. Para ella es un privilegio tratar de interesar a los niños en el mundo por medio de sus libros.